SECRETS ON HOW TO HAVE A SUCCESSFUL MARRIAGE

Proven secrets for building a happy relationship

Kelly Winston

TABLE OF CONTENTS

INTRODUCTION

There will always be challenges involved with committing to someone for the rest of your life. Although there is no simple formula for a successful marriage, some couples appear to have it down. Their trade secrets include having sex, supporting one another when they go their own ways, and, of course, communicating constantly. You'll find some tried-and-true advice for marriage success in this book.

CHAPTER 1

THE FUNDAMENTAL ACTIONS TO TAKE

People frequently confuse pure love with unconditional affection. When they first meet the people they want to spend the rest of their lives with, they always claim that they will love them no matter what, but after a few difficulties in the union, they would leave and turn against one another. It is not what love and affection means; rather, it refers to a "Mother's Love"—a mother's love for her children that endures no matter what difficulties or difficulties they may face. No restrictions, constraints, or circumstances apply to unconditional love. When you care for someone unconditionally, you don't expect anything in return; all you want to do is support, love, defend, and take care of them.

Your love for your family members is genuinely unwavering because no matter what, you will always remain as a unit that cherishes and upholds one another, even if you are all split up and have your own families. The parents' love for their child is the epitome of unconditional love. Whatever issues arise—their test results, a disagreement, a deeply held conviction, or actions they make that change their lives—their love for one another is unwavering and constant.

If you care for a buddy without expecting anything in return, that is also seen as unconditional love.

Giving someone you are not blood related to your unconditional love is difficult because if they make even one mistake, your faith in them will be lost, and it is difficult to love someone you don't trust. You should discover the fundamental stages to make your love life count if you are in a relationship and want to improve it.

You'll be able to live a prosperous existence if you are aware of the crucial steps to making your romantic relationships count. You will have challenges as you move through life, and if you can't deal with them effectively, your relationship will undoubtedly deteriorate and eventually end. Sometimes it takes time to fall in love again, especially if your previous relationship was serious and you ended it.

Even the knowledge that your ex-partner is content with someone else stings. However, individuals need to be aware of this truth. No matter what suffering you endure, life must go on. You have to have faith that everything occurs for a reason because love is a marvelous thing. So if your relationship didn't work, you can be confident that a better person is soon to enter your life.

CHAPTER 2

EXPRESSING UNCONDITIONAL LOVE

You should start loving yourself if you want to show your family that you love them without conditions. There is no such thing as having to demonstrate your ability to love unconditionally; you simply need to do it.

How can you love everyone without condition if you can't even show them that you love yourself? If you know how to handle situations appropriately, when you are patient, kind, and you know how to forgive and forget, you can easily demonstrate your unconditional love to everyone.

Someone who also loves himself is capable of receiving unconditional love. You must love yourself in order to get unconditional love. When you give this kind of love, it can be felt spontaneously, thus there is no concrete proof.

People can tell from the beginning if they are receiving unconditional love or not. If you have an unwavering love for someone, you would do everything for them. You love them more than anything in the world, so you don't want anything in return.

Regardless of how difficult things may be, you can wait patiently because your love is there. A mother's love has no restrictions, no requirements, and no bounds. No matter who they end up being, you always accept and adore your children. Regarding genuine, unwavering love, you are prepared to wait patiently for the appropriate moment when your child will feel the same way about you. Similar to how you can tell whether a relationship between two people is truly unconditional if both of you feel the same way about each other. You can only demonstrate your unconditional love; there is no way to express it in words that are precise. If you feel that you have this unwavering love for someone, it signifies that you are willing to endure pain and suffering in order to demonstrate your devotion to them.

CHAPTER 3

KNOWING WHERE TO DRAW THE LINE

If you are overly dependent on your romantic relationships, you will eventually suffer. Being overly dependent on someone or something is also harmful for you since you will struggle to move on and confront reality once it is gone. Being linked to someone also implies that you are completely devoted to them and cannot imagine your life without them. You will feel the weight of your sorrow once they are gone or no longer under your control, and it will be difficult for you to go on. That explains why so many individuals are letting their love lives or excessive depression take over their lives and make them uncontrollable. If you want to experience unconditional love, you must figure out how to let go of your attachments in relationships. You will be freed from misery and obligations by letting go of all your attachments. You will be able to break free from your restrictions and express yourself freely if you can learn to love without conditions.

It takes a lot of guts to enter a relationship since you are aware that as the connection develops, there will be many challenges you must overcome. Because of the lessons you will gain from these hardships, you and your relationship will grow stronger as a result. But you shouldn't allow yourself to become emotionally attached to these errors because doing so will just make you feel inferior and diminish your self-esteem. Start with yourself if you want to learn how to cut the ties in your romantic life. You will be able to adapt to your position with ease if you fully control your emotions and are aware of your limitations. Additionally, it’s critical that you keep an open mind so that you may consider all the advantages and regain your composure. You may overlook other things that make you happy when you are so committed to your partner. Your entire universe is focused on that one individual, so when they depart, it seems as though everything has come to an end. You should try to break free from your romantic bonds because this is a bad emotion that you should aim to avoid. Always think about going out on your own and doing what you enjoy or what makes you happy while you’re by yourself.

CHAPTER 4

HOW TO DETERMINE IF YOU HAVE A STRONG EMOTIONAL CONNECTION

Everyone wants to experience the wonderful feeling of receiving unwavering affection. Your parents love you unconditionally, of course, because they already do. If you also deserve to be loved, you can experience unconditional love from someone you love. Everyone want to know unwavering love, particularly from their parents, as this is what defines or creates a person. Some people are hesitant to love unconditionally since they did not receive it from their parents. It doesn't follow that you should treat your children badly if you were one of the children who didn't know unconditional love due to your unpleasant history.

Since you already know how it feels, there is no purpose in denying your children what has already been denied to you—unconditional love. A crucial element that establishes the basis of wholesome interpersonal and intimate relationships is emotional connection. Therefore, it should unquestionably be highly appreciated. Even if we may have everything else we require, a lack of an emotional connection can be a barrier to pleasure and satisfaction in a relationship. Couples that become emotionally estranged from one another have a gap that cannot be filled by lavish presents or admirable deeds. Therefore, it is crucial for both parties to maintain the emotional connection. The good thing is that you can always try strengthening the connection if you think it's fading. Some methods for reestablishing the emotional bond with your partner have been covered in this book. The telltale indicators of a relationship with emotional ties are listed below.

1) **PERIODIC ASSESSMENT**
   Partners that are emotionally linked frequently internalize their relationship and identify areas for improvement. Speaking your mind honestly is rarely or never hesitant.

2) **DEEP UNDERSTANDING OF EACH OTHER**
   People who are emotionally attached are conscious of every tiny characteristic that makes their partner unique, from being aware of and embracing each other's imperfections to having a profound grasp of each other's personalities. This entails being aware of their concerns, driving forces, principles, aspirations, and weaknesses.

3) **THERE IS A SHOW OF PATIENCE**
   Patience is one of the essential elements of a powerful emotional relationship. The best indication of an emotional connection is when both of you consistently display

patience, even when the other spouse is being challenging or unreasonable.

4) YOU BOTH ENCOURAGE ONE ANOTHER

Sincere support is crucial for developing a strong emotional bond. Depending on the needs of each person, this support may be physical, emotional, or mental.

CONCLUSION

It is extremely crucial and cost-free to show unconditional love. You will undoubtedly find the ideal mate in the globe if there is this kind of love in the world. You can only find that person when you learn to love them unconditionally. You need someone you can trust, rely on, and spend the rest of your life with. Always keep in mind that to love unconditionally is to do so with all of your heart, without any reservations, restrictions, or limitations. Marriage is a difficult endeavor. It takes time, work, and maturity to build a solid marriage. But it's worthwhile. If you want to learn how to have a happy marriage, using the marriage tips stated above will always need almost all of yourself. The majority of the fleeting pursuits we make with our life are less valuable than a happy and successful marriage.

www.ingramcontent.com/pod-product-compliance
Lightning Source LLC
LaVergne TN
LVHW080559160826
845677LV00010B/1923
* 9 7 9 8 8 4 7 6 7 4 4 5 4 *